TENDERMAN

OTHER BOOKS BY TIM BOWLING

Low Water Slack (poetry, 1995)
Dying Scarlet (poetry, 1997)
Downriver Drift (novel, 2000)
The Thin Smoke of the Heart (poetry, 2000)
Darkness and Silence (poetry, 2001)
Where the Words Come From: Canadian Poets in Conversation
(editor, 2002)
The Paperboy's Winter (novel, 2003)
The Witness Ghost (poetry, 2003)
The Memory Orchard (poetry, 2004)
Fathom (poetry, 2006)
The Bone Sharps (novel, 2007)
The Lost Coast: Salmon, Memory and the Death of Wild Culture
(memoir, 2007)
The Book Collector (poetry, 2008)
The Annotated Bee & Me (poetry, 2010)
In The Suicide's Library: A Book Lover's Journey (non fiction, 2010)

TENDERMAN

TIM BOWLING

NIGHTWOOD EDITIONS

2011

Nightwood Editions
P.O. Box 1779
Gibsons, BC VON 1VO
Canada
www.nightwoodeditions.com

Cover design by Carleton Wilson
Printed and bound in Canada on 100% post-consumer recycled,
ancient-forest-free paper, processed chlorine-free and printed with
vegetable-based dyes

 Canada Council Conseil des Arts
for the Arts du Canada

 BRITISH COLUMBIA
ARTS COUNCIL
An agency of the Province of British Columbia

Nightwood Editions acknowledges financial support from the
Government of Canada through the Canada Book Fund and the
Canada Council for the Arts, and from the Province of British
Columbia through the British Columbia Arts Council and the Book
Publisher's Tax Credit.

Library and Archives Canada Cataloguing in Publication

Bowling, Tim, 1964–
    Tenderman / Tim Bowling.

Poems.
ISBN 978-0-88971-259-1

    I. Title.

PS8553.O9044T44 2011   C811'.54   C2011-904672-5

for Levi, our youngest,
whose working life will hopefully contain
considerable dignity and freedom

CONTENTS

I grew up in a blue-collar town ten minutes down the road from a white-collar town. And I've spent most of my life uncomfortable in both places. But my fundamental loyalties remain with those for whom the world of wealth and influence is as remote as space.

The Tenderman, then, represents a kind of savagely independent working-class Everyman, a figure increasingly pushed to the margins of our homogenized society. He's not a Romantic figure, however. He's not even particularly admirable. I've spent the past eight years addressing him (sometimes I call him Rosie, sometimes I write as if he's me) and yet he seems to recede further and further, gone into that pulsating grave of spirit where most wild species have also gone.

I wish him well, and thank him for his unintended gift of several metaphors and dramatic situations. But true to his nature, he doesn't want my thanks or anything else. Unlike Greta Garbo, who actually said "I want to be left alone," the Tenderman wants to *be* alone. As if on a deathbed without the presence of death. In a world without metaphor.

After eight years, I'm finally ready to leave him there.

TIM BOWLING
Edmonton, Alberta
August 2011

Tenderman

TENDERMAN: *official name for a crewman on a salmon packing boat*

Are you out there counting in the mast-light's dim
as the back-eddy swirls the yoked boats down
and fresh numbers strike to plunge the corks?
Are you keeping careful track of the dead?

One hundred and twenty-seven sockeye,
forty-six humps, a big pig of a spring
like a full collection plate
in a starving parish – tell these
to the packer. He'll scrawl them
in his book, along with total weight,
then tear the onion-skin receipt
out to give the setter of the net.

Are you hosing down the decks of blood,
the tip of your gaff, the soles of your boots,
and lighting a smoke as you take in the stars?
When the fisherman speaks, do you know who he is?
Do you know that he and his deckhand are dead?
Add two. Hook them under the ribs with your pick,
sigh for the extra work. Unyoke.
The stern-rope slimy in your hands
as if you'd pulled a gut from Time.

Tender the Indian. Tender the Jew. Tender the Chinese dissident.
Tender the crawling over the face of the earth
and the flying through the air
and the feeding in the wood,

tender the wild, tender belief,
tender till your shoulders burn
and the count and the weight
are the earth and the sky
and the packer writes your name
with the toe of his boot
in viscera, your life,
our lives, the pitiable years

    of these, tenderman.

THE TENDERMAN'S PRIMER

See the salmon run. See them die.
Pierce their gills with a pick.
This is Level 1.
You are ready for work.

Now see the salmon go extinct.
No blood, no slime on the deck
or caked on the sides of your boots.
No sockeye, coho or pink.

You have advanced to the highest level.
Smallpox squirms on the river blanket.
See the past. Keep it alive
as long as you have breath.

You are ready for death.

STUDY: CANOE PASS

In the sky, one moon, full.
On the river, one salmon boat.
In the cabin, two men, sleeping.
In the stern, 27 salmon, dead and dying.

Why don't you paint this, tenderman?
Leave out no detail.
On the hands, 7 cuts, 215 scales.
On the alarm clock, time.
On the eyelids, salt.
In the veins, blood.

It should be easy.
The heron's already set up his easel in the marsh.
His blue paint's wet. Start with the eyes of the men.
It doesn't matter that they're closed.
You've looked into them often enough.

On the drum, one torn net.
In the engine, gas and oil.
In the heart . . . what?

Use your imagination. Reality requires it.
Come on, hurry up . . . Too late.
All your subjects are in motion
and they're never going to stop
in just that pose again.
Paint them now, tenderman,
and you're painting light with shadow,
you're painting the leaves that have fallen.

In Place of the Lyrical Irish Night

A fast tide. With the net out
we slide along the bank
like a pat of butter off a boiled cob.
Mosquitoes can't light on our bared arms.
The boat's a burned-out comet;
we teeter on a permanent brink,
passing blackened canneries, a blur of farms –
all around us, magnified a millionfold,
the lapping of a parched dog
and salmon cracking like iced branches
between the corks.

Twenty-five years ago, tenderman!
And I never thought it was a life,
it was just a job.
Perfection of the life or of the work.
William Yeats, a poet, told me that,
whispering off a page one night
where the gangly heron not the gliding swan
gulps down fathoms of the oily dark.
Now I would perfect the past
that wasn't perfect – and for what?

The tide runs out, we pick the net,
we roll it on the drum, make another set,
the tide drops, goes slack.
The sun comes up and daubs the wings
of the obese bluebottles on the salmon's blood.
Heat rises, cloys. A glut of men and boats
settles on a river the colour of dung.

We walk from cabins to decks
lifting our sticky boots. We blink.
Our lashes catch on salt and a spume
of crimson flecks.

Squint. Pat the day's dead dog.
Pick, pen, or gun, get on with the job.

BRITISH COLUMBIA

Wake up, tenderman. This is our stop.
The past – where the unhappy take their honeymoons.
Somebody ought to toss confetti at a severed foreskin.
Or at least fold tears into a pocket handkerchief
for the Regret Chest.

See that schoolyard, those boys
playing cat's cradle with the intestines
of a garter snake? Ebenezer, old friend,
these ghosts are us.

The iron maypole chains flay the overcast.
A girl with an impetigo scar
tosses a stolen medical bracelet
in a hopscotch square, and leaps.
Can you guess who the teachers are?
Also us. Sighing over bad coffee,
and dreaming the honest report card:
Susie's a little prig who could use
a good swift kick in the ass.
Brian's thick as a doorpost.
Don't send this school any more of your brats.

The rain falls. Suddenly.
As once did the contents of the chamber pots
upon the stony mews of our heritage.
Everyone runs for cover.

But there isn't any, not really.
Before us, through us, and after us,
the flood.

All aboard, tenderman.
We've got a train that runs
on Chinese bones
to catch.

The Tenderman's Brief History
of the Late Twentieth Century

Quebec threatened to separate, we killed the salmon.
The last chopper left Saigon, we killed the salmon.
Someone took a potshot at the Pope.
Someone winged the President of the States.
Someone plugged a Beatle.
We kept on killing the salmon.

The computer came into the home,
many people on cellphones stopped
using words like "cripple" and "Indian,"
they lined up at bank machines,
they swiped cards and burned CDs,
they taped shows to watch them later,
unreal shows about reality,
highlights of the wars for oil,
they camcordered the birthday parties
and the weddings (never the funerals),
and we killed the salmon.

Some of the salmon we killed
were made of chemicals and plastics
and raised in pens
and they died listless in our nets.
There weren't as many of the other kind,
but we killed both.

Children went to daycare in plastic diapers,
pre-school care before school opened
and after-school care after school closed.

The wharves and the streets were mostly clear of them . . .
for fear of sexual predation
and fear of accident
and fear of the deadly random . . .
the fields and riverbanks were mostly clear of them.
Less seen and less heard
they watched DVDs in mini-vans
and had scheduled times to play.

By the end of this period
we hardly ever killed the salmon,
we rarely got the chance.
But the salmon died, keep dying.

It is hoped we will someday reach Mars
and walk there
on the planet stained with all the blood
we did not spill, that eluded us –
evanescent, drifting ether,
wilderness.

U.S.S.R.

History's amusing when it isn't simply murderous.
Once there was an Iron Curtain, and your
beard hair, Rosie, was Soviet red
when you heard that splash in the rain
and did your bit to part the fold.

(My Reading was Unsupervised, Sustained, and Silent.)

He spoke a sailor's polyglot in gasps
once you'd yanked him from the current
and fixed him a spiked mug of tea. Comical.
A free man who rarely opened his mouth. A Pole
who'd jumped ship to exuberant utterance.

(I sat in my place in the row of desks
behind streaked window glass
reading *No One Here Gets Out Alive*
and *Down and Out in London and Paris*.)

You couldn't tender that blowhard fast enough.
The pleading eyes, like a mother seal's
whose pup you'd clubbed. The neediness.
You gave him warm clothes, some cash,
nodded toward Vancouver as you idled at the Steveston dock.
History's unremarkable when it isn't downright murderous.

Hell knows, there's little irony awareness
in authority, but I learned to chuckle behind that curtain
(Unsupervised, Sustained, and Silent)
as your lips kept their horizon, your eyes morsing

surveillance of the motionless corkline
while the Pole hand-dragged his anchor chain
of family, friends and memory, all over
Lulu Island slippery as frog skin.

The tide ran out. The teacher looked up.
Time for another set, another class,
another headline about freedom.

History's banal when it isn't simply murderous.

AFTER A TRIP TO THE MUSEUM AND ARCHIVES

Old-fashioned things, tenderman. Handwritten letters and
childhood, things we have no time for,
what our mothers called "common courtesy,"
friendship, full sentences, recovering
from illness. Make for me a shroud
of all that's spinning in our wake,
the local store and sportsmanship,
any object made of wood, the face-
to-face encounter, decorum
concerning intimate matters, appropriate dress
in public, Sundays off, any work
that can be cancelled by the weather.

We must be getting old, tenderman
(sangfroid at getting old).
Tenderman, what other clock
should our midnights face?
My shadow bag clatters
with discarded cogs and wheels
and gears turning amongst feathers
handpicked off pheasants
and shoeboxes stuffed
with photographs that didn't
turn out as we expected,
which are the truest images
after all, for what turns out
intact to our conception?

Inter me, tenderman,
with the blown-glass flaw

a child with absolutely
nothing to do
picks up
on his solitary way
to nowhere.

Now We're More Apt to Whisper the French of Proust to the Baby in the Womb

Dipstick. Peckerhead. Fuckwad. Numbnuts.
It isn't exactly a gentle rain, your tongue,
is it, Rosie? But still I fall asleep to it
some nights when I can't believe my father's dead
and isn't climbing the dyke with dripping ingots
soldered to his wrists. Sonofabitch.
Prick. Jesus H. Christ. Mouths open
back of smoke and stars, half the time
in anger, half in laughter. Jerk-off.
Ass-wipe. Cocksucker. All the wharf-patter
I wouldn't want my kids to hear, I hear
a thousand miles and a world away
with smiles sometimes giving way to tears.

I won't shit you, you friggin' retard,
English was my mother tongue
before I was fobbed off on the schoolyard
with its silly anthems and subtler cruelties.

Sometimes at night I still cry for my father.
Clear water sprung from a filthy river.

WHARF RATS

I was never one of you, tenderman. Never.
Not when Wiggy paid in sockeye for buggery
in the blackberries behind the netshed
or when crazy Pat Brophy hung off the net rack
by his testicles (because he could, you bastards)
or when the morning's first heron
served its platter of fine bone china to the sun.

I stood only on the edge of your truancy,
attracted and repelled, staring through glasses
fashioned by a timid oculist. I stand there
still, rain on my lenses, as you toss down
the dirty stained mattress
to hump the girls
not-quite-right upstairs
and laugh like panes of glass
rock-shattered in the condemned houses
encircling our town like the tents of a circus.

I was never stung, tenderman,
by the whole hive of place.
What you brushed off, I picked up,
the stingers and sudden corpses
of summer. The shards
in the nursery of the stillborn.

Whispers the jittery oculist,
"Kid, can you read the top line of death?"

TIME AND TIDE

Were you ever happier, tenderman?
Two days without sleep, the catches huge,
the river slack at last and
almost closed for the season,
you were about to be removed
from consciousness, but fought it
out of the pure delight
of knowing you had emptied the net
of summer's riches. Outside,
salmon bones brittled the oak
and maple leaves, the nights
revolved on rims of frost, the boats
waited slaughterhouse-cattle thick
in the harbour. If you slept
too soon, you'd lose the pleasure
of smelling the potatoes frying
in the pan, of hearing your father
ask your mother for a second cup
of tea, of feeling the armchair's
mild swell, if you slept too soon
you might wake
to a river that never opened,
to an absence of salmon,
a silver hole in space,
to dead voices whose timbre
was fading, a buoy-bell struck
by a killer whale's sounding
for depths suddenly shallows.

Tenderman, what is this happiness
constructed on so frail a thing
as the earth and those
who labour in it?
Yet you were happy once,
we were happy there,
fighting sleep with youth,
counting the earnings
of muscle, even as
silt filled the veins
of those we loved
and the bones snapped
in the spawned-out leaves
of the sorrowless oak
and maple.

A LITTLE SONG OF CARNAGE

Once I was asked to be tenderman.
The count of the dead too high for one.
The packer saw the mortal moth
hover at my numbering mouth.
The count of the dead too high for one.

I found I didn't have it in me.
I didn't have the guts for guts.
I counted red when the flesh showed white.
I gaffed the flesh when I sought the gill.

At last the packer bid me,
"Count the Arctic char."
"The Arctic char? There are no Arctic char."
"Now you're cooking with gas," he said.

Sometimes in sleep I hear the click
of the pick on the abacus bone,
feel the warm rain sluice down
from the cold grey gut,
wake and shiver and wait
for the sharp descending prick.

Once I was asked to be tenderman.
The count of the dead too high for one.
The packer saw the fragile moth
flutter back of the look of youth.
The count of the dead too high for one.

CURTAIN CALL

What applause did we ever get, tenderman?
The kicks and slaps of a hold of dying fish –
hands in an auditorium
restless in a thousand laps –
and the red confetti of the slaughtered drake
over the sun-ruddied marsh.
But what praise does a worker want
except his work? To rise in the dark
and tie his apron on, no promise
but the same expense of skill
and sweat, the sun that warms
your body and also rots your catch,
the seagulls flung off our shoulders
so many dead letters to their office?

Read this by the light of a cupped match.
That isn't the sound of cheering, tenderman:
it's history at the day's dry pool
still trying to slake an ancient thirst.

One Who Made the Tenderman's Wage

Ten words exchanged in ten years, and never hello.
"That it?" And a jab with the pick at the drum.
Chain-smoke? They could have bound Houdini
a hundred times over with that length of iron.
A lazy eye that somehow
made you see the salmon's gape
again, or the film of indifference over the moon.
Once, flipping a three-foot sturgeon onto the scales,
the barbs raked his forearm, and six times
he snarled "Fuck!" at twenty-second intervals
while blood constellated the deck. Make it four words,
the curse being general, aimed at the work,
the pain, the life, the all
of the flesh he was in. Six-two, rust-bearded,
he drank alone on the same bar stool all winter,
his right arm attacking the pints like a pick.

"That's it," was all I ever said back.
But thought "Fuck" six times when I heard he was dead.

BEEKEEPER AND TENDERMAN

One wears a mesh headgear and gloves
and blows smoke into the hives,
the other a ballcap and a Harley Davidson
T-shirt one size too small for him
and draws smoke into his lungs.

One is nonetheless immune to stings,
the other curses daily at the sturgeon's raking barbs.

One climbs toward a wild swarm in the apple branches
a grey monk ascending a bell tower,
the other leaps from deck to deck
a Great War soldier in a soundless film.

One knows the honey that's made from each nectar,
the other can guess the exact weight of death.

I would have them meet in the fall
when their craft is at its ebb, the air still,
and shake hands, and without talking,
a quietus make
in the dripping super of the stars

for the moon their eyes have worn like a lens.

WE WALKED OUT EARLY TO MURDER THE SUN

We walked out early to murder the sun,
returned with warm chamois of light at the belt.
But the sun never died. It glazes the paper edifice,
this blind of words and years
built to hunt what can't be killed
because it's not alive. Why crouch here, then,
frost in the joints, dew on the lashes
and the old relentless leaf-fall in the chest?

I know your answer, tenderman,
the vinyl that plays your song.
You would never say, with me,
when is the quarry never the self,
the cocked gun not regret or pride,
when is the sunlight cold
in the black interiors of the barns?

Shh, be quiet, Bud, you say,
and raise your arms, and tense,
and kill us both again
through the blind

with silence.

WALKING THROUGH A NORTH AMERICAN CITY, THE TENDERMAN PICKS UP A RHYTHM

Conform (Do your own thing) Conform (Do your own thing)
Something sinister in the schoolyard
The sky's the colour of spider-catch
Do your own thing (Conform) Do your own thing (Conform)
Down at the parlours, tattooing fresh meat
Down at the parlours, tattooing fresh meat
I Love Mom on a joint and a hock
I Love Mom in the rib of an eye
Conform (Do your own thing) Conform
Nobody's got any time for Time
The astronomer hasn't got any space
I got a sad letter from a childhood friend
so I emailed him a couple of lines
I got a sad letter from a childhood friend
so I emailed him a couple of lines
Will you be buried or will you be burned?
Conform your own thing conform
Will you be ashes or food for the worms?
Be your own cancer conform
Do your own stroke conform
Will you be ashes or food for the worms?

Man is in chains before he is born.

Happy Hour in the Arms

The old man didn't so much as teach me
how to fish and mend net and gear. I watched
and he figured after a while I'd know
how to do it. Fished on my own at ten,
the old man passed out on deck, a 26er
of rye snagged in a suspender, the prick.
But he cared about me, I'll give him that.
When he whacked me, I had it coming, mostly,
jacking off when I should have been paying attention.
You can't be a kid on a river, there's
too much going on. It's a place for men.
So I had to be one. That's about it.
School? Nah, I couldn't wait to quit.
And I figure I've made a damned sight more
than you over the years, with all your university
and shit. Even after I started to tender
and made just a percentage of the catch
it was a good wage. So now it's dried up.
What am I going to do, cry about it?
The job's not coming back. The government
doesn't know its ass enough to wipe it.
But yeah, it's a shame, eh.
The river at night in the fall. I remember
this one time. I was – I don't know – fifteen maybe,
and I'd just finished setting on the Prairie
when I hear this big splash off the bank.
What the fuck? I turn around. In the moonlight
nothing but the head and antlers, must have been
a six-point buck, and he's swimming like hell
to get across to the marsh. It's so quiet

I can hear his breath, a kind of rasp,
but his head's completely still, like
it's made of rock. I never even thought
to grab my gun. He just kept sliding across,
the current taking him down. I figure
he hauled up somewhere by the town clock (*laughs*).
If one of the Gibbies got him, I never heard the shot.
Seems like a long time ago (*laughs again*).
The good old days. Don Bemi
used to send his season's sockeye money
home from Rupert in the fucking mail.

(*Shakes his head. Gets up from the table.
On the way out, pays*).

Monologue

Remember the croak of the heron at first light?
The terror and then the delight?

Remember that mountain of power we had to climb sideways
on broken footing, in downpours, hands baked or numb always?
I thought that was a peak we'd never even see. Now it's razed.

Were there more stars then? And yet the dark was darker.
Whatever god there was wasn't keeping his fleet tied up in harbour.
Darkness now's like something dragged through muddy water.

You see, I try so hard but I can't get it back.
Not that I even want to, but it's the knowing that I can't . . .
And forty more years would be lucky living with the lack.

I don't expect anyone to understand. Age means loneliness
and coming to terms with the utter coldness of death.
Of all the days, said Virgil, the first to flee are best.

Outside, the moon over the harbour clenches its bloodless fist.

NATIVE CITY

English and no apologies, tenderman.
Hell, the place was named for an English sailor
(not Hell, smartass, Vancouver).
Even the nicotine-stained yellow polar bears
flopped on cement in the Stanley Park Zoo
knew that much: their ancestors,
after all, watched Franklin (another
old salt from the old sod) and his blood-poisoned crew
drag a sled of Victorian bric-a-brac
over the frozen wastes
(which were frozen but not wastes) to their deaths.
And that bay where the hippies in our childhoods
flogged macramé and all their tie-dyed crap?
You guessed it: English.

That's right, Jack. The world's
whitest and unsexiest heritage,
ankle-high socks in brown sandals
toad-in-the-hole mushy peas
Royal Doulton on our mothers' cups
and crusty old blighters who'd never
buy anything made by the Japs
on account of how they treated
prisoners of war in the war camps.

Stiff upper lips?
You don't know the half of the half
of it. I doubt Marcus Aurelius
himself was any more stoic.
You really had to hand it to them.

Or else they'd just take it, bloody sailors
sailing around like so many Adams
naming every place we'd ever have
a memory, except the odd Salish
town that escaped their tongue: Tsawwassen
and . . . and . . . well, I forget
the others. But then, I'm English,
tenderman, just like you, whelped
by the bitch, Anglo, abandoned
by the bastard, Saxon,
born to spit the pips
from our coxes
as we cycle the village green
on our way to see the sexton,
heads high, Empires lost,
our pant legs neatly clipped.

GOING TO WORK

Pre-Dawn

The ground mist like a butcher's wax paper
shreds. Autumn, the roast's blood,
seeps through. It's quiet. The cowled spider
at his bell-rope sleeps.

Daybreak

The street's a chewed leash. All dogs are loose.
Each bark brings a mallard down.
In the marsh, the narrow sloughs,
the flat punts glide. The light's dim.
Standing fathers cradle newborns
like shotguns. Already, on clotheslines
hooked from kitchen windows to smokehouse roofs
the wrung dishrags of the flock
drip on rotting windfall pears.
The neurons of the hornet
circle the electrons of the wasp.

A man's the packer's scale. Each death
adds weight. But who pays that price?
Tenderman, shovel on the ice.
The shoulders have to bear cold, too,
along with the dog salmon's taste.
I'm my own son on childhood's street
pulling the triggers of dead leaves.
But Time's already murdered

everyone I knew. The coloured photo
in my pocket's turned black and white;
it shows a girl in a cherry tree
before the booze and forced abortions,
it shows a man with a cigarette
before the lung died on the vine,
it shows a boy
grinning through the grave-dirt.
But it's not necessary
to look at anyone's past
to see your life. What's between
the blossom and the rot
is variation, and we've been there
enough to know the sameness.

Noon

The air's a rungless ladder
Death keeps pulling up behind us
until, even with ourselves, we're alone.
The potholed street plunges down
between blackberry bushes hung
with spiderweb. To walk here's
to pass a row of winter windows
against which the children
of the poor smudge their breath.

Then comes the lot with the solitary maple,
the cenotaph the women built
without civic help –
charred body, hands tearing roots out
and gore-spattered telegrams

slipping from the first widowed moment again.
When children play here
they're at the top of a rigging
carved from the bones of family pets.
We're close to their sea-struck reverie.
From here, it's only a fathom to the dyke
that kept the water but never the river
from our sleep. The tide fingers its rosary.
Listen! The itinerant knife-grinding gull
begins a mocking faith of buy-and-sell.
Now we have to climb. Our muscles
and the plates of earth engage. The sky
above is God's numbed skin
we slap and slap with presence. The channel
below is grey, the gone-silent gull
hangs trembling a foot above the surface,
a beating heart torn from a corpse.
We keep it beating, become that pulse.

A cedar log set in the bank – the pheasant breast of it.
The ants' penmanship, the woodbugs' moorage – visible life
and so many dead within, same as the planet.
But there's no time to rest. In the mud and rushes
a skiff like a worn saddle. We throw it
on the rippling flanks, and drift.

The net in the bow . . . a net? Or
the glazed mulch of autumn, a sick,
soaked dog? Touch it. The caked blood
sleeps on the sills of a thousand windows
as we open them and lay them out
till a glass wall stands in the current.
To fish without the hope to kill

is to live with deeper hope.
But life's in abeyance. Death's
pewter blows attack the hull.
Along the far bank, the deadheads shift
in one direction, artillery trained
to the coordinates of Heaven.
Stand. Smoke. Be as still
as the spine-bone wrapped
in the blue shroud of the heron.
No word from the arm-weary tenderman.
He stands like an uncarved totem
in the cooling molten. It's left to us
to carve the face on him.

Late Afternoon

The sun sags, a doorstep pumpkin,
no expressions now except goodbye.
The net's full of silt, we drag it
like a broken wing behind us.
Smoke rises along the dyke
where unimportant people burn
their most important papers – smudge pots
to keep the nattering life away.
The river's already partly ocean,
bones are showing in my photographs,
the tenderman's cutting his own face;
it bleeds, but soon
a billion brilliant scars
will shine against the onyx grain.
Tell me something true of yourself,
the air insists, the air that's made

of owl-breath and blowhole vapour.
And what can you say,
what can I say, what
can we say, except
I was a child and now
my hands are headstones
for every embrace I never gave?

Night

Slick as horse flesh in the rain, the ocean.
And the thunder of hooves below . . .
what's coming is what you're here for.
The moon lifts its pale hand,
wipes away a dirty tear,
is suddenly gone. Black of volcano rim.
We're looking down, all of us,
lifelines throbbing.
What strikes the net strikes us.
No one speak. Do the work
of the death that's ours.
Haul in. Tenderman,
no pity now, no ice.
One thousand salmon to pick,
crack of voltage, your life . . .
heave into it, last chance,
each breath torn from the throat
like a leaf.

Midnight

We were never promised this world.
Where are you now? Drifting.
And in your hands
the stilled lead of pendulums,
on your skin,
cold sweat off the brow of God.

WHILE TRYING TO GET THE GEAR IN GEAR

Taken from the concise chaos of the river
the salmon's regal script punch-pressed
through silt and oil, taken
from our father's delicate strokings
of the lissome willow's hair
untangled from drift nets and held
(as if they readied
the princess of the story
for a kiss), we were taught
to regiment letters along lines
and to enclose all colours.
Why not? Doesn't every stem
of a flower keep tight its green?
The black of the salmon's eye
doesn't run, not even if you plunge
a knife blade in – it's like the night
before the first adolescent rage
at the injustice of mortality,
taking, taking, and still looking back.

If you are fourteen and cursing the stars
as you try to outrun the tide at your elbow
does it mean some god
has broken his crayons
and dashed the inkwell from the desk?
Is each salmon a shard or a goblet hurled
whose final smash has never come?

A shout blossoms along the dyke
between Chung Chuck's potato patch
and Cal Leatherbee's Home Oil tanks.

Was it meant to be?
Must the world always take us
from us? Fathers leaning over
for a cold kiss, the daughter
of the river's broken spine
and melting flesh . . .

Shit, sorry, Rosie. Got a little carried away there.
Hand me that fan belt, would you? Thanks.

Please Do Not Disturb

Most of my friends are dead writers.
Even worse, they're poets. Tenderman,
is this normal? The conversation's quiet
and mostly in metaphor, which means
everything is something else, and
isn't it true, after all? That sockeye
you just flung off the pick to the heap
with a slap – was a live fish,
dead flesh, and now cold cash –.
in only a matter of seconds.
Metaphor's just a word for life,
nothing to be afraid of, or laugh at,
unless life is. And if it is,
well, I want to talk about it
even with dead poets. Would
you take that bottleneck
out of your mouth? That's
what I mean. No conversation
here over the guts and the brine
which are so much more
than guts and brine . . . are
the ephemerae of the task
of the sun's ascension . . .
ropes and tears, ropes and tears,
in the bell tower scaffolding.

As you crack the cap between your teeth
I hear my good friend's pelvis snap
on the river ice at Minneap
and rush again to the parapet
and span of his pages.

Even reading alone is something else,
a shout, a prayer . . .
but I won't say life is death,
not even to my friends. Tenderman,
look at that heap of fish . . .
if all it can be is a pile of coin,
hook your pick
to the chords right now,
swing me to oblivion.

HERE

The fleet was a rope we let out from the town.
Faith made that fibre, the salmon
rung the bell, seals rose around us
in their monks' cowls, eyes wet
as the palms of Christ, life dangled
in the full abyss. And the town –
where the side of the sleeping dog
and the soil of the backyard garden
rose and fell in the same rhythm –
was held to the earth by laundry lines
and street lamps and the anchor chain
of shops – where the beekeeper's veil
and the Greek widow's veil
leaned over the smoke the river kept
between its banks, everyone trusting to
the docility of God in the aftermath
of His will – that town was guy-roped
with the cat's cradle of loneliness
in the schoolyard and the trellis
of torn seine net for the sweet peas
behind the undertaker's parlour and
chalked pool cues laid down for a fight
in the Reef and the Arms. And it held
for a hundred years before the rot and the fray,
it was pulled in slowly, season by season,
as the creekbed called the sockeye
and the queen bee her workers
and the top of the fir tree the tired heron,
with the same song behind the pulling,

of music never to be questioned,
notes that are heard only by doing . . .

Yesterday I stood in the side yard of my time
in the grass wet with dew and blossom-flecked
and stared at the dead salmon
my father had laid there before
he climbed the wooden stairs
and opened the cracked door
and did not look back again;
and I stared at the still bee on the gill
that learned death was no nectar
and broke off the erratic writing
before she signed the hive with love.
Until now, I didn't know what silence was.
Until this moment, I wasn't aware
of the broken rope and the chafing
in my palms that,
to the utter indifference
of the world of towns,
keeps the seal's eyes supplied
with a swimming pity
for the meaningless, vanishing ardours of man.

Seminar at Ladner: Moby Dick

So does he ever catch the fucking thing or what?
Ah tenderman, Coles Notes for the docks
does not exist, there's no such help
for life. Salmon scattered about
in the shadows of the childhood home
like panes of glass blown out,
the tiny streaks of blood the bloodshot
that comes from looking and not seeing
what once was lived with joy.
Haven't you noticed
the flanks of every dark
flash white
as they roll across the earth?
Tenderman, it's because
the story's so simple
we complicate with meaning.
All sorts of things are caught,
forgotten, fixed in our forgetting.

Tell me whose leg isn't part of this dock.

An Hour of Twitter, Texting, Facebook and Thou

Tenderman, tenderman, what to do?
When everyone seeks celebrity
the proper aspiration's
anonymity. But of course
you're famous for it.
Look up Nobody
in the Book of Life
and there you are,
not there. Like
the author of Beowulf
you're known
only for what you did
not who you did it with.
Friends? I have to laugh.
There's Pain, Spit, the Dark
on the River and eventually Death.
This text isn't short enough
for your screen. Once,
drunk, mad, and cardless,
you crashed your truck
through the bank glass
to trash the ATM.

Tenderman, let's go back
to childhood, that thin glass.

Can I be your friend?

REAL MEN READ JANE AUSTEN

Testosterone, tenderman?
We always had too much of it.
At best, the surplus went
to consensual sex
with various sluts or to cold-cock
that goon who patrolled the point
for the Pillars Inn. At worst,
it went to raping and killing,
bodies dumped in ditches and posters
peeling off telephone poles
in the wind, even here
in the precincts of melancholy
invisible to the rain's soft foot patrol.

As a child I listened for hours
to the crabs in the ceramic pot
of boiling water on the stove
as they scrabbled to escape,
the sound that engraves the heart,
history's bony hand at the lid of the crypt

and watched the blood of the Greek
wife-beater's wife drip
into the flour for the pastries
that reminded her of home,
the wine-dark waters that circled her eyes.

It goes on . . .
My sensitive ten-year-old son
can somehow in anger even think to call

his mother a fucking bitch
drawing from the well
of the hateful culture
in which we live.

Like a cooked crab, tenderman,
I reach in vain for this –
after a half century
to settle in with a sigh
to a few hours bliss
with the masculine prose of the feminine.

Are You Contemporary?

Who brings a gun to a knife fight, tenderman?
The age is without class. I would
with the little white man at the intersection
like to vanish and then come back.
But it won't be done.

Supper tonight and tomorrow's
a plate of blue-eyed peas.
I feast on all I've seen.
The heron, like a beer stein,
leaves when it lifts a ring.

For those who flunked
the School of Hard Knocks
I offer enrolment in the past:
the bowl of fruit on the table
the shadow of the bowl of fruit
on the table the bowl of fruit
on the canvas. Your first test:
where will the blowflies settle?

This coffee's not instant, tenderman,
this food isn't fast. If you flense
the whale of life with only haste
you're using a dull blade, boyo.

I have decided to do no work
unless I'm asked. My work is poems.
It wouldn't pay Thoreau enough to live at Walden
Pond in 1848 and he cut slow and sharp.

Oh but the beautiful
uncut hair of graves
Walt Whitman called the grass.

DESPAIR, OR THE TECHNOLOGIES

The world is too much, tenderman, soon and sooner.
Edward Dahlberg said, "Our cult is the new,
we would slough our skins every day
if we could." The butterflies are where?
Pinned to the aesthetes' powdered eyelids.
To beguile the time,
look like the time,
urged the lady with the hygiene of a raccoon
as she uploaded the murderer's
detachments and set the salmon to spawn
on the skin of the sleeping grooms.

Ah tenderman, who would be an antiquarian,
the trembling meat in the piranhas' aquarium?

Better to be the absence of honey
in the throat
of the tenor. Is this an iPhone
which I see before me? The lady looks
daggers.

COURAGE

You had to be Greek to go up the Greek slough.
And even then, tenderman, even then.
If you were the wrong kind of Greek . . .
you know what I'm saying. From Corfu
instead of Crete, outside the parea, wearing
the wrong club colours, worrying the worry beads
when you didn't have a worry
in the world. Better set your net
on another drift: try Finn Slough.
The Finns aren't likely to slit
anybody's throat in the street
after dark, in a gang, or even alone,
not that we ever knew any Greeks
who actually put the blade to the bone
of a man foolish enough
to go up the Greek slough; it was just
the thought that the thought
could occur to them, revenge straight
out of Aeschylus, or wherever it is
that cold dish was first served.
Tenderman, tell me, who else ever put
so much violence into the way they spat?

Might as well simply state the facts:
our family's first boat was the *Nautilus*
which we bought off Jimmy Tassis.
For a whole summer my father left
the faded Greek flag on the mast
because no man was ever less

interested in nations. Even so,
even with that standard flying
and the sockeye rumoured
to be choking that drift,
my father wouldn't risk
going up the Greek slough.
Some things, in some places,
a man just wouldn't, just doesn't . . .

And yet didn't I kiss
with my eager Anglo mouth
untouched by olive oil, octopus
or ouzo, at least three
of the seven daughters
of Demitrios Polymenakos,
the seven wonders
of the ancient
which was the modern
and thus the only world?

Give me a sultry August morning
off the wingdam, a mouth
full of cherries sucked clean
to the pits, and twenty years
waking like whale sperm
from my rudder. I'll turn
the wheel and head straight
for the black Hellenic fire,
I'll go right up the slough
where my brothers and father –
all my own parea – wouldn't go.

The joy of the joy of joy.

Tenderman, my tender flies that white and blue.

TELLING THE TENDERMAN'S BEADS

Gillnetters in crushed gravel drives, linen web hanging
from the black limbs of the Bing cherry,
boats and nets in motion behind trucks
of rattling rust, the rain falling, the eyes
of salmon staring out from
blackberry bushes, a heron
swallowing fingerlings of mist and shivering
(Ichabod Crane in the Hollow
tubercular seminary student)
the union leader on the gallows
of the blood-brocaded wharf collecting
dues, the Japanese cannery man on the sandbars
plunged on the sword of his shadow,
a seal checking her skin at the edge
of the human, a poor woman bargaining
for a cheaper cut of the rain,
the scarlet under the mallard's wing
meaning death the scarlet under
the blackbird's wing meaning flight
a shed door thrown open on the scent
of fresh-cut cedar, a laundry line
dripping with a whole infield's uniforms,
hydrangea azalea forsythia
the full moon's skullcap of cloud,
the sea, near and far, alcohol of longing,
the chalk outline of a child's body on a sidewalk,
the bag of rosin on the pitcher's mound
in the dark, a pod of abandoned houses
choked by the hard plankton of stars,
seventeen lit ends of cigarettes

at anchor, the crab shell
like a discus in the girl's hand
on the shingle
where she walks her song

my failure to hold and contain
to convey my failure to make
that spiderweb is bone
every fathom of rain
with its own thin rib-cage
the poet's a coughing spider
who drains his heart
a woman's hand withdraws
from a drape, more rain,
a cracked yellow bulb
over a flaking door
moths circling
gumboots on the porch
dew and dried blood on the rubber
my outlines and my interiors
unfading life, fading art.

BARNBURNING

Not anymore. Nobody cares enough
to wound a man in his rot. Tenderman,
remember the cornfields washing right up
against the wood, remember childhood,
beer parlours and the wooden match? I hold
the husks. Where are the unsheathed blades?
If we were Japanese, we'd fall on them.
Look to the west. That could be Swenson's barn
crackling on the horizon if it wasn't the sun,
if this wasn't another August without salmon.
Why not? Somebody getting even
might have crouched in the corn
with a gas-soaked rag for the straw,
somebody might still have thought
it was a way to hurt, as this is –
run through the scorched stalks
at the edge of the main event, brother.
Don't look back. Time's squinting through the sights.
The pop of the kernels is gunshot.

POSSESSION

Time to come clean to the cops, tenderman.
We had it and it got us high awhile
behind the bleachers at the fastball diamond
in the bloodstained faceoff circles
of the lacrosse box when we should have been
in remedial math class or comatose on the couch
watching reruns of *Bridget Loves Bernie.*
But it's been a long time
since we came down, a long time,
and the side effects have lasted years.

Did we deal? To whom?
Everybody had the same supply.
That junk was as easy to score as the stink
of sour silage in the air. If you were there
you got your ass hauled down to the cop shop
for just breathing. And why not?
Breathing and a heartbeat
were the hydroponics of the stuff.
Back then, living was our only grow-op.

Now you have to add memory to the mix
and the cops don't even care.
It's medicinal and almost legal,
we've got it to the full ten tenths
of the law, we're out there dealing
and buying from ourselves.

And there's nothing this shit won't cure.

LAST WILL

You don't have any children, tenderman?
No one to pass the hopelessness on to?
Don't be proud. It's no great victory
to end your road at the address
you boarded up with the planks
of hulls that never leave harbour.

I stand with my three at your door.
They have no idea why I've come
or why my heart beats wildly
at their playful knocks.
It is all Halloween candy to them,
our past of tides and salmon
weighed carefully as newborns.
How can they die before they've lived?

A wind that we called a westerly
when it mattered to our skill
blows in the door. One after
the other, like letters delivered
decades too late, the children slide in.
It's like that game we used to play,
Red Rover, Red Rover,
except no one's calling, no one's coming over.

The next house is as warmly lit
as any gillnetter's stern
on any dark set
we ever made, tenderman.
And the next, and the next.

But I have no desire to cut
my lines and drift.

And if that means for us
empty hands untangling emptiness
the moon's tired labour on the tides
then let's be men talking to men, at least.

Between the fathers and the childless,
this coupling to give stillbirth to lies.

BETWEEN MEN

Tenderman, what common ground?
Wordsworth – you wouldn't know him –
wanted to be a man talking to men.
But without manhood,
there's nothing to say –
only images: a heron's wing
dripping blood
a loaded bough of cherries
the last salmon of the season's
lockjawed expression
on the season's first
jack o' lantern . . .

A parking lot
behind a strip mall
northeast Edmonton
refugees of the Sudan
slaughter a kid goat
the crackling smoke
obscures
the industrial towers.

If I squat on my haunches
with a hunk of greasy flesh
in my hands
and talk to you, tenderman,
without irony, of the past,
will it be direct enough
for the lost children of Darfur
to overhear

as their eyes delta blood
and each bite builds a village
that each swallow tears down?

What men? What words?

Whose soul grown deep like a river?

WHAT KIND OF MAN ARE YOU

tenderman? I know,
you are not like the others.
You don't wear scent. For you,
technology's an axe or
an engine and confers
no status. The idea
of watching other men play sports
would never occur to you.
Pussy, douchebag, bitch: the culture's
lazy misogyny; it's a foreign
language even though you
can translate it. You have
never wanted attention; most
men you would scorn
if you ever gave them
a thought. I know this.

But what kind of man are you?
It's a form of self-asking
for I am not like these either,
and yet, between us, tenderman,
rivers marshes
starscapes bloodstreams
all the killed and the being
killed species of longing.

What creature are we, then,
who sees the bridge
of our escape
and does not want to cross it
and does not want to destroy it

but only watches each night
the sun touch the steel
as autumn invades the salmon
at its bone?

BLAME

The knives are out for us, tenderman,
that I thought we'd put away.
But now the blades glisten
with our blood not the salmon's.
The world says it's your fault
the fish have gone, though
yours was not the greater profit.
And I am scorned for translating
my hatred of power
into verses.

Tonight along the Fraser
the dark's viscera still hangs
off the star-hooks though we do not wipe it
from our throats and brows with slimy burlap
or stuff it slowly into every daybreak's
slitted mother-of-pearl. The headlight beams
of the joy-ridden Audi sink in the tide
like milt. The stereo spills a song
from the year of the last big run
onto the log boom cedared air.

The knife in the glove box –
sharp, the finest steel –
guts only the murderer.

If, As Science Tells Us

If, as science tells us,
all the greenery in the Yukon
springs from the deaths
of the salmon in its rivers,
what will grow from your grave,
tenderman? What green
will rise to heaven out of the humus
of your sweat?

Beg pardon. *Our* sweat,
what will ever bloom of it,
this scything
shoulder blade
and temple writhing
with the old chrysalis

except (look up at the sun
        look down at the river)

more of this?

JUDGMENT

Please rise, tenderman.
What have you to say for ourselves?
That we were children inside childhood
as hunger inside the wolf
milk inside the breast?
And that now we are men inside manhood
dead wolf and dry breast?

In the snow, in the heavy snow
of the middle years, the snow
that melts as it falls, white nectar
that feeds the reflecting self,
we receive our sentence:

to be taken from this place
to an appointed moment in the naked future
and executed by breath and pulse
until we are only and entirely past.
Until then, we are condemned to be no happier
than a single moment in sunlight decrees
or under a gibbous moon, paused,
the body a hand in the palm of its wonder.

For the crime of seeking to make public
this private, uninhabitable ground
so the High Court of the Hard Look
writes without pity, in stone.

Tenderman, take us down.

Death Beats Us Up the Drift But We Can Always Cork Him

Only one boat of the old fleet's
still moored in the harbour. There's
no new fleet. The boat's owner's
in a home a thousand paved
fathoms from water. The blood's
still ringing in his wrists but the world
won't answer. He's dying,
like us all, of inoperable
longing. Do you ever visit, tenderman,
the chill side of your shadow
where it floats on the slack?
What dream do you taste, what flock
and what kill do you covet
huddled all-seeing there in your blind?

Once, several selves ago,
I flicked on the lights
in an empty warehouse
and felt the rats disperse
the dark as if they bore it
on their backs. And so,
the rising moon,
this river and these salmon,
replicate the switch, the empty space, the rats?

No dice, tenderman. The mind will touch
again the world the dying held.
And I will play the antique Roman
falling on the faint reflection
of my shield.

ENVOI

You must be dead, Rosie.
I didn't see you at the Games
lungs bursting for gold. But then,
as they say, silver's the first loser,
and our whole past is silver.
At least we owned the weight
around our necks
and it pointed our faces at truth –
no scoundrel's refuge for the man
who works hard for his dying.

Dead, you're alone on the podium
rotting from the inside
like any country or politician.
Power doesn't turn its mic to you
for a quote on courage
Wealth doesn't want to know
how much you scorn its lily wastes.

You stand there on a wharf
of slime, scales and creosote
singing the anthem of the registers
without a false note, raising
two fingers, one for the lie
that is God, one for the lie
that is country, and then spit
on the worthless corpse
of your own clear sight
before the river sweeps it away.

You've trained so hard for this.
And all your life. No support
from anyone and no applause
except the blood falling in waves
on a hard, white shore.

Tenderman, it's beautiful to be alone
on our own dead water
with Charon when his hood comes down.

ACKNOWLEDGEMENTS

A selection from *Tenderman* earned the author a fellowship from the John Simon Guggenheim Memorial Foundation in 2008 and a grant from the Canada Council for the Arts in 2006. Thank you to the juries of both competitions. The following individuals are also honourary Tendermen (yes, including the women): Philip Levine, Russell Thornton, William Heyen, Nola Bowling, Don Domanski, Don McKay, Silas White, Norm Sacuta, Tom Flanagan and Anne-Marie MacDonald, Dorothy Jean Bowling and Theresa Shea. Five of these poems previously appeared in *Fathom* (Gaspereau Press 2006); thank you to Andrew Steeves and Gary Dunfield for the permission to reprint them.

About the Author

Tim Bowling has published nine poetry collections, three novels and two works of non-fiction. The recipient of four Alberta Book Awards, a Canadian Authors Association Award, a fellowship from the John Simon Guggenheim Memorial Foundation, and several other honours, including two Governor General's Award nominations, Bowling lives in Edmonton. In fact, just like the tenderman, he has never lived anywhere other than British Columbia or Alberta, and never farther than a half-mile from a major river.